AF469379

This book belongs to:

... ...

Flora, Buxton & Bear

POORLY FLORA visits the DOCTOR

Rowena Blyth

Today, Flora is feeling really poorly, so her friends, Buxton and Bear, visit her at home to try to cheer her up.

“I’ve brought you some of your favourite, juicy strawberries,” said Buxton.

"Thank you Buxton,
but I can't eat strawberries...

...my throat feels like it has a **prickly**
hedgehog stuck in it," said Flora, glumly.

"I've brought you these beautiful flowers Flora," offered Bear. "They smell *lovely!*"

"Aaachooooo!" sneezed Flora.

"I can't smell flowers, Bear.
My nose isn't working and it feels
like it's being tickled by
a million **feathers.**"

"Well, what about this cover to help keep you cosy?" asked Bear, as he wrapped Flora up in a huge, thick blanket.

“No, thank you, Bear. I’m **so hot,**
I feel like I’m in the desert
under the boiling sun,”
complained Flora.

“But then,” said Flora,
“I feel **all shivery** and cold,
like a little penguin on ice.”

Buxton and Bear didn't know how else
they could help Flora. But then...
"Flora!
It's time to go
to the doctor!"
called her mummy.

At the doctor's surgery, Flora sat in the waiting room, listening for her name to be called.

"Flora Fox, to see Doctor Warren in Room 3 please,"

said the receptionist over the speaker.

Flora sat on a big chair and the friendly doctor got out her special bag of instruments.

She looked into Flora's mouth with a torch...

...she checked her ears with an otoscope...

...she took Flora's temperature with a thermometer...

...and she listened to her chest with a stethoscope.

"You've got a cold Flora," said Doctor Warren.
"Take this medicine, get plenty of rest,
and you'll feel better
in no time."

Back at Flora's house, Buxton and Bear came to visit to see how she was feeling.

"I still feel horribly poorly," said Flora quietly. "I don't think the medicine is working."

"My mummy says that laughter is the best medicine," said Bear.

"I have an idea!" said Buxton excitedly.
"We'll put on a funny show to make you giggle,
and then you'll feel all better!"

They dressed up as clowns and hopped on one leg...

...but Flora didn't smile.

Buxton climbed on Bear's shoulders and sang a song...

...but Flora didn't laugh.

They even juggled with jelly!

But it was no use. Nothing seemed to work.

Until...

...Bear tripped over, throwing Buxton into the air!

Buxton crash-landed onto Flora's toys and the jellies went

SPLAT!

Flora smiled...

and then giggled...

and then laughed **hysterically!**

"Thanks Buxton. Thanks Bear," said Flora.
"I'm feeling so much better already!"

But then...

"Aaachoooooo!"

sneezed Buxton.

"Oh no!" gasped Flora.
"I think we're going to need
some more jelly!"

Other titles in the

Flora, Buxton & Bear

Leap Book Library

www.fourthwallpublishing.com

First published in Great Britain in 2018 by Fourth Wall Publishing
Copyright © Fourth Wall Publishing 2018
ISBN: 978-1-910851-61-6
All rights reserved
www.fourthwallpublishing.com
2 Riverview Business Park, Shore Wood Road, Bromborough, Wirral, Merseyside CH62 3RQ
A catalogue record for this book is available from the British Library
Printed in China